WANDSWORTH

EARLSFIELD and SOUTHFIEI

A Portrait in Old Picture Postcards

by

W. J. Drinkwater and P. J. Loobey

S. B. Publications

First published in 1993 by S. B. Publications
c/o 19 Grove Road, Seaford, East Sussex, BN25 1TP

ISBN 1 85770 035 X

Typeset, printed and bound by
Redwood Press Ltd., Pegasus Way, Bowerhill, Melksham, Wiltshire,
SN12 6TR

CONTENTS

CONTENTS

CONTENTS

THE AUTHORS

WILLIAM DRINKWATER lived and worked in the suburbs of Southall and Hornchurch for fifty years. After serving in the RAMC for the duration of World War II, he held positions with various London contractors and City firms before moving down to Corsham in Wiltshire where he now lives in retirement.

Bill (an avid collector of old picture postcards and cigarette cards) has been widely published in magazine articles on an extensive range of subjects, including disablement, military matters, local history, short stories and collecting hobbies.

His recent book *Southall/Norwood, A Portrait in Old Picture Postcards*, published by S. B. Publications, was released in 1992 and takes a nostalgic look at the area in which he grew up.

PATRICK LOOBEY, born in 1947, has lived in Balham, Putney, Southfields and Streatham – all within the London Borough of Wandsworth. He joined Wandsworth Historical Society in 1969 and has served on Archaeological, Publishing and Management Committees, being Chairman of the Society in 1991 and 1992. Having collected Edwardian postcards of Wandsworth Borough and the surrounding districts for 18 years, he has a wide-ranging collection encompassing many local roads and subjects.

Patrick has privately published a volume of postcard views on Putney and Roehampton in 1988 and another on Battersea in 1990. Reproductions of all the views in this book are available from: Patrick Loobey, 231 Mitcham Lane, Streatham, London, SW16 6PY (081–769 0072).

INTRODUCTION

This book is an illustrated history of Wandsworth, Earlsfield and Southfields, as seen through the medium of old picture postcards. It is the combined work of two men – both ardent collectors of old postcards – and comprises just a small selection of Patrick Loobey's extensive collection to his annotations, and introduced and compiled by William Drinkwater, a prolific freelance writer on the postcard and local history scene. Both authors readily pay tribute to the many postcard publishers, printers and photographers of yesteryear without whose work and expertise this book would not have been possible.

For those who are not familiar with the area, perhaps the best place to start a perambulation is Wandsworth Common, a large open space of some 183 acres surrounded principally by good-class houses, which extends in a southerly direction from Wandsworth Town towards Tooting. Wandsworth Common has suffered more in the past from encroachments than any other Metropolitan common. It was acquired in 1871 by a body of conservators from Earl Spencer, the Lord of the Manor, when numerous enclosures threatened to swallow up the whole area. In 1887 the Metropolitan Board of Works took it over. Then it was a bare place, muddy and sloppy after rain, undrained and almost devoid of trees. Today it is a pleasure-ground, well planted with trees, a richly-wooded lake and other attractions. The Common is divided into two parts by the tracks of British Rail. One portion was once the resort of gipsy vans and tents.

On the west side is the Royal Victoria Patriotic School, erected as part of the scheme for the relief of families of soldiers who perished in the Crimean War. The building, a free imitation of Heriot's Hospital, Edinburgh, was designed by Mr. Rhode Hawkins and the foundation stone was laid by Queen Victoria on 11th July, 1857. To the north is the Emmanuel School for boys.

Between Trinity Road and the Railway track is Wandsworth Prison, built in 1851, then to accommodate a thousand criminals. It is mostly used for prisoners undergoing sentences for burglary and robbery with violence, including smash-and-grab raiders and motor-car bandits. Adjoining the prison, between Earlsfield Station and Magdalen Road, is the Wandsworth Cemetery.

Earlsfield only came into existence with the late Victorian developments that followed the building of the railway station. Before this time the centres of population were Summerstown and the hamlet of Garratt at the foot of Burntwood Lane. Even up to the First World War large fields of allotments stretched between Magdalen Road and Burntwood Lane and a dairy farm was still operating in the 1950's from the area surrounding Garratt Green.

Wandsworth is, of course, named after the River Wandle and is a corruption of Wandlesworth, meaning the village on the Wandle. At the close of the eighteenth century, Wandsworth became a resort of Huguenot refugees, whose burial ground on East Hill contains many notable names. In the High Street are the palatial Wandsworth Municipal Buildings, consisting of three storeys built adjacent to the Town Hall, a less pretentious edifice and, opposite, the local Technical College. All Saints Parish Church near the bridge over the Wandle, dates from the end of the eighteenth century. To the south of the High Street is King George's Park and Recreation Ground, which skims the west side of the River Wandle and extends for half a mile towards Earlsfield. Near the entrance to the Park is a large open-air swimming-pool provided by Wandsworth Borough Council.

Doubtlessly places change over the years and Wandsworth, Earlsfield and Southfields are no different to other London Boroughs in this respect. However, the greater the change the greater the interest in things of yesteryear . . . in what things used to be like in the world that has passed in the mist of time. Nothing brings back memories of the days of yore and reveals the transformations the district has undergone, as well as old pictures. It is hoped that this collection will appease the appetites of older residents, satisfy the curiosity of many new ones and encourage further research by others.

None of those who know the area today, or knew it in days past, cannot, one feels, but be fascinated by the array of nostalgia presented between the covers of this book.

High Street, Wandsworth, c. 1913

Looking east down West Hill from the top of the old fire station. West Hill Library and Convent of the Sacred Heart are on the left.

High Street, Wandsworth, looking west. c. 1912

The sixth entrance on the left is the old Wandsworth Technical Institute. The 18th and 19th century buildings on the left were demolished in the 1920s to make way for the present Technical College. The buildings on the right were demolished for the present Town Hall in 1923–24.

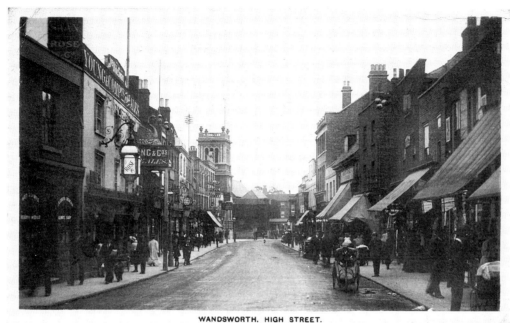

High Street, Wandsworth, looking west. c. 1908
The narrow road was widened in 1919–20 and The Old Swan public house on the left was demolished in 1924 for Alan Taylor's Motorworks.

High Street, Wandsworth, looking east. c. 1906

A quiet lunch-time scene. Whitby Builders on the left are now in Church Row. Also on the left, selling cycles, pianos and furniture, are Cresswell & Ball. The canopy over the pavement on the right is still in place, being the entrance to the Spread Eagle public house. Behind the boys on the right can be seen meat in the open in the butcher's shop. Also of note is the old Town Hall built in 1882 and the horse-drawn 'bus from Putney.

High Street, Wandsworth. c. 1908

Photographed in Garratt Lane facing north, notice The Ram Inn and Tap House. Young's Brewery building in the background dates from 1883, but a brewery has actually been on the site since 1675. Stimpson's building on the left was demolished in 1968 to make way for the Arndale Centre. The tram is not numbered, but a system of three coloured lamps was used to denote the route – see above 'Plough Road' (Battersea) and destination board.

High Street, Wandsworth, facing east. c. 1926

The Wandsworth Borough News building on the left is still going strong. The Ford building in the centre was built in 1924 on the site of the Old Swan public house.

High Street, Wandsworth, looking east. c. 1926

On the left is Putney Bridge Road. On its way to Tooting Broadway is a no. 77 'bus. To the right of the 'bus is Hardwick's Department Store which closed in the 1960s. Feed and hay merchants, Anstee & Co., on the right, closed in about 1980. It was not an uncommon sight to see bales of hay being loaded onto lorries and vans and, unfortunately, there were a few serious fires in the large hay-shed at the rear of the premises.

High Street, Wandsworth, facing east. c. 1924

On the left can be seen the Palace Cinema. On the right, beyond the no. 28 tram on its way to Willesden are recently demolished buildings (1924) (note the hoardings). A comparison can be made between this view in 1924 and No. 4 in 1906.

Wandsworth Technical Institute, High Street, Wandsworth. c. 1928

Work on the foundations started in 1923 and the building was opened in November, 1926 by the President of the Board of Education, Lord Eustace Percy. The cost of the work was £70,000. The building was later enlarged by 108 ft. along Wandsworth High Street and opened on 3rd December, 1936 by the Duke of York (to become King George VI). In the background is the Two Brewers public house.

High Street, Wandsworth, facing west. c. 1918

The Bull public house on the right was bombed during World War II. All Saints Church has been rebuilt several times – the tower brick exterior in 1630, north aisle in 1724, nave in 1780 and chancel in 1891. During World War II the tower was partially destroyed and was rebuilt in 1955. The tower core is probably 14th century. The buildings on the left are in the process of demolition for road widening.

The Baths, High Street, Wandsworth south side. c. 1913

This rather distinctive building (Architect H. Spalding, Builder Walter Wallis of Balham) was opened on 6th July, 1901 by John Lidiard, the First Mayor of Wandsworth and demolished in 1968. Buckhold Road was diverted and now (1992) covers the site.

West Hill, Wandsworth. c. 1930

'Any more fares please?' asks the conductor of the no. 35 General Omnibus on its way to Highams Park. Palmer's Newsagents on the left, also had a hairdressers as part of the shop and, in addition, carried out umbrella repairs. The Police Station on the right was built in 1883.

West Hill, Wandsworth, looking west. c. 1903–06

The Catholic Church of St. Thomas of Canterbury on the right with the tower still to be added. On the left is the L.C.C. Fire Station which was destroyed in a bombing incident in November, 1940 with the loss of six firemen.

Upper Richmond Road, facing west. c. 1908

Note the barrel-organ on a two-wheeled cart being operated by two young boys. Suffolk Hall on the left was originally built as a public house but never obtained a licence and has remained as showrooms or workshops ever since.

The Aquaduct, Wandsworth. c. 1912

This was built across the Wandle Valley to carry the southern outfall sewer towards the Kent coast and was demolished in 1968. The view is from Merton Road facing east with Buckhold Road in the foreground behind the caption. King George's Park has not yet been laid out on the green here. At the far end of the grass land are Garratt Lane and the River Wandle.

The Council House, East Hill, Wandsworth. c. 1928.

S 7222   L. B. & S. C. RAILWAY STATION, WANDSWORTH COMMON, LONDON

Wandsworth Common Railway Station. c. 1910
Built for the London, Brighton & South Coast Railway Co. Note the beautifully tended flower beds – a familiar sight on
railway stations at that time.

E. G. WARWICK.
RED LION,
YORK RD,
WANDSWORTH.

WINES & SPIRITS
OF THE FINEST
QUALITY.

BACK. & FRONT.

Red Lion Public House, York Road. c. 1908

Formerly known as Red Lion Street and now (1992) called Ram Street. The building stood at the rear of Young's Brewery and the brown glazed tiles of the pub form part of the brewery wall to this day. To the rear of the pub was McMurray's canal which ran from the Thames almost to the High Street. This was originally built in 1801 for the Surrey Iron Railway and filled in during the 1920s.

Prince of Wales Public House, Summerstown. c. 1908

Built in 1852 to serve the growing hamlet of Summerstown in Garratt Lane. Rebuilt in 1898, but badly damaged during World War II and the decorative rendering above the windows has now gone. Notice the fine view of two Young's Brewery drays and the publican standing on the pavement between the barrels.

Royal Patriotic School, Wandsworth Common, looking east. c. 1915

In the forefront of the scene is the Clapham Cutting signal-box.

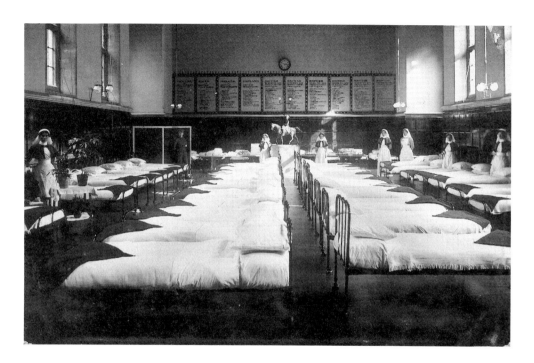

Royal Patriotic School. c. 1917

The Receiving Ward prepared for casualties. An interesting point is the bronze of Lord Kitchener on horseback at the far end of the hall. The grounds of the school were filled with tents and as many as 1500 patients were here at one time. During the Second World War it was used as a Processing Centre for refugees from Europe and many apprehended and convicted spies were taken just over the road to Wandsworth Prison to be hanged.

Royal Patriotic School, Wandsworth Common.

Visit of King Edward VII and Queen Alexandra on 24th July, 1907 to commemorate the Jubilee. The King unveiled a tablet in the entrance hall to mark the visit. Also attending were the Duke and Duchess of Connaught (President of the Royal Patriotic Fund) and James Wise, Mayor of Wandsworth. The 'Royal Victoria Patriotic Asylum' was built as an orphanage for children whose fathers had died in the Crimean War. The foundation stone was laid by Queen Victoria on 11th July, 1857. Taking two years to build, it cost £31,337.

Wandsworth Firemen, West Hill Station. c. 1906

In the background can be seen the horse-drawn steam appliance.

Stn. Sgt. Syme.   P.C. Palmer.   P.C. Caryer.   P.C. Hook.   P.C. Osman.   P.C. Browne.   P.C. Sutton.   P.C. Westrip.

P.C. Cooke.   P.C. Hawkins.   P.C. Smith.   Insp. Martin.   P.C. Johnson.   P.C. Cosh.   P.C. Waight.

P.C. Bean, (Capt.)   P.C. Mantz, (Vice Capt.)

WANDSWORTH COMMON POLICE FOOTBALL CLUB, 1907-8.

Wandsworth Common Police Football Club 1907–8

WANDSWORTH BAND

Wandsworth Salvation Army Band. c. 1906

"Wandsworth". 1906.

Postmen's Sorting Office, St. Ann's Hill. c. 1906

The building still stands, but the Post Office Sorting Depot is now in Twilley Street. The number of postmen employed, as seen in the picture, would account for the numerous deliveries and collections – around five each day – at the height of the golden age of postcards.

Wandsworth Borough Band and Committee. c. 1906
In the background, Wandsworth Gas Works in Fairfield Street.

Emanuel School, Wandsworth Common. c. 1908
Diligent pupils with teacher in the Engineering Workshop.

Morrison & Fleet Dairies Milk Cart. c. 1906
The depot was situated at 1 Station Parade, Southfields from which milk and cream had to be delivered once or twice a day.
There were, of course, no refrigerators in the majority of local houses until the 1950s.

The Upper Mill from the original Buckhold Road. c. 1905

The Wandle, in the early 19th century, had over forty mills. The Arndale Centre now stands on the site.

The Welsbach Incandescent Gas Light Co. Ltd. factory in Broomhill Road, Wandsworth, facing south. c. 1906
Gas mantle manufacture was a major industry in Wandsworth. The building is still in existence.

Austin Willis & Co., Replingham Road, Southfields. c. 1908

An abundance of wares fill the shop windows of 'Southfields Leading Drapers'.

Freeman, Hardy & Willis shoe shop, 119 High Street, Wandsworth. c. 1915

The postcard was sent by Alice, the lady in the doorway. Working in the shop was one other lady, a boy and a gentleman called Walter. 'The World's Smartest Footwear' and 'Anatomical Shapes' were promised if you purchased your shoes from this shop. Note the prices – 4/11d. to 7/11d. for men's shoes with some footwear priced at over 10/-d. (50p).

Llewellyn & Sons, 22 East Hill, Wandsworth. c. 1915

Six shop staff and two delivery boys were employed by this small family grocers (really a provisions shop). Prices in the window on the left include Spanish Port at 1/6d., Invalid Port 2/6d. and Rum and Whiskey 3/6d. On the pillars to each side of the windows see the patriotic posters 'Men of the Empire TO ARMS!' and 'Our Brave Soldiers at the Front Need Your Help'.

Spooner's Laundry, 82 St. Ann's Hill, Wandsworth, founded 1871. c. 1912

An advertising photograph, possibly taken to show off the two new motor delivery vans. Probably John and Charles George Spooner standing by the horse-drawn vehicle on the right.

THE FAMOUS FACTORY.—FRONT VIEW.
FRAME FOOD Co., Ltd., Standen Road,
SOUTHFIELDS, LONDON, S.W.

Frame's Food Factory, Standen Road, Southfields, facing south. c. 1906
This company produced baby food – note the inscription 'Nourish and Flourish'. Actually, the green tiles on the factory wall face are almost Art Deco. The building still stands (1992).

36

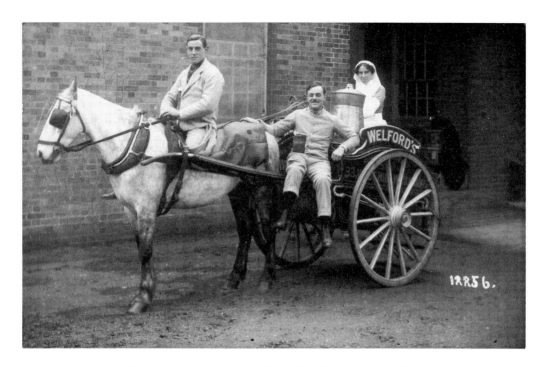

Welford's Dairy Cart, 33 West Hill, Wandsworth. c. 1915

Both soldiers wear the pale blue uniform issued to convalescents in First World War hospitals. The soldier on the horse has had his left leg amputated. A posed photograph with nurse and two patients, probably taken at the Royal Patriotic School, Wandsworth Common, which became the 3rd London General Hospital in World War I. Welford's had extensive farms and dairies in Surrey and South West London. In the picture is Cart no. 46.

Southfield Evening School Football Club Team 1906–7.

W. Crouch, corn and seed merchant, of Wandle Granaries, Earlsfield. c. 1912.

Central Hall Picture Palace and Ice Skating Rink, East Hill, facing west. c. 1912

Built in 1909 for the new vogue of motion pictures, but this leisure complex closed in 1918. Notice the admission charges to the Picture Palace – stalls 3d., balcony 6d., children 2d. and 3d. respectively.

The Lyric Picture Playhouse, Wandsworth High Street, facing east. c. 1919
Built 1912 and closed 1934.

The Picture Palace, Earlsfield.

The Premier Electric Theatre, Garratt Lane, Earlsfield, facing east. c. 1914
During the 1960s this cinema showed mainly Indian films, but it later became a Bingo Hall and was demolished about 1987.

SOUTHFIELDS' RIFLE CLUB.

Collins, Southfields.

Southfields Rifle Club. c. 1902

Sited off Granville Road on the south-east side of the railway embankment. A silver cup was presented to the club by Councillor Dawnay in 1909 for a rifle-shooting contest.

St. Barnabas Church Fete, Southfields, 1925
Note the decorated bicycles and fancy dress worn by many of the children.

No. 1172.   SOUTHFIELDS:—THE RAILWAY STATION.

Southfields Railway Station. c. 1910

Built by the London & South Western Railway Co. and opened in 1889. British Rail own the track and station but only London Underground trains stop here.

No. 1168. SOUTHFIELDS:—THE RAILWAY STATION.

Southfields Railway Station, facing south towards the main station building. c. 1910
In the picture is a London Underground train on its way to Mansion House. Thousands alight here during the Wimbledon Tennis Fortnight.

No. 1171.　　　　　　　　**SOUTHFIELDS :— AUGUSTUS ROAD.**

Augustus Road, Southfields, facing west. c. 1910

Southfields was still being developed and open farm land is still on the left (notice the stack of hay in the field). The Bank buildings and houses on the left came later.

No. 1120.　　　　　　　　　　SOUTHFIELDS:—REPLINGHAM　ROAD

Replingham Road, Southfields, facing east. c. 1910

A quiet scene with the only traffic being a hand-cart for bread deliveries and two hand-pushed dairy carts (completely different from the very busy road of today). See also the shop blinds down to protect the merchandise on display in the windows.

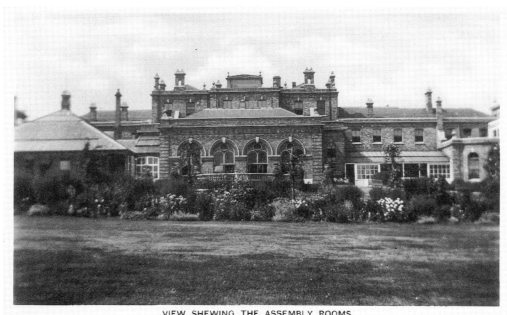

VIEW SHEWING THE ASSEMBLY ROOMS.
ROYAL HOSPITAL AND HOME FOR INCURABLES, PUTNEY

Royal Hospital and Home for Incurables, West Hill, Wandsworth, looking north. c. 1920.

No. 1167. SOUTHFIELDS:— CORONATION GROUNDS.

Southfields – Coronation Grounds c. 1912

Of note are the ankle-length boots on the boy and girl, also the white pinafores on the children, worn to keep their other clothes clean (but how did they also keep the pinafores so spotless?).

Wimbledon Park Road, looking south. c. 1910

Not a person in sight apart from the two men working in the field on the left with horse-drawn grass mowers.

THE WANDLE WEIR WANDSWORTH

The Wandle Weir. c. 1912

In the background is the Waggon and Horses public house in Garratt Lane. The site of the Mill probably dates back to the Doomsday Book or earlier. In the 18th century the site was occupied by Easton's Paper Mill and later by Henkell's Iron Mill where cannon was forged and drilled for use during the French Wars, i.e. 1805–15. It subsequently became known as McMurray's Paper Mill which had a disastrous fire on 17th January, 1903, throwing 160 men out of work. The building was used by Benham's Engineering Works until the 1980s and then replaced by modern industrial units.

Earlsfield Station and Garratt Lane, looking south. c. 1910
The sign on the lamp post was a 'stop' for tram cars.

Earlsfield Station. c. 1906
Signboard states 'Earlsfield and Summerstown'. The line to Wimbledon was built by the London & South Western
Railway Co.

Earlsfield Road, looking east. c. 1906

These fine three-storey houses were erected during the 1880s. The boys with cricket bats are probably on their way to play on Wandsworth Common.

Garratt Lane, Earlsfield, facing south. c. 1920
J. Slater's Haberdashery still had the beehive sign above it into the 1960s.

Aboyne Road, Garratt Green. c. 1908

Children posing in their knicker-bockers and pinafores. The land behind the gentleman on the left was farmland with dairy cows into the 1950s.

LOWER TOOTING:- GARRATT LANE

Garratt Lane, Summerstown, looking north. c. 1908

Burmester Road on the right with the Prince of Wales public house, post office and Harry Cusden's stores in the background. Disastrous bombing in World War II removed all the shops on the right.

EARLSFIELD: GARRATT LANE

Garratt Lane, Earlsfield, looking north. c. 1908

On the right is Wilna Road, on the left is Lydden Road, also the Jolly Gardener and the Grosvenor Arms public houses. A busy scene, but one cannot really imagine the man standing in the middle of the street today.

Garratt Lane, looking north. c. 1912

Earlsfield Station in the background. Earlsfield only began to grow up around the railway station during the 1880s. The older village was near the Leather Bottle public house (see No. 64).

GARRATT LANE, S.W.

Garratt Lane, looking north. c. 1908
The large building on the right was the L.C.C. Board School. An interesting mixture of bicycles, trams and horse-drawn vehicles.

Garratt Lane, looking north. c. 1908

Isis Road to the right. This scene would be virtually impossible to reproduce with the children today due to the amount of traffic.

Earlsfield Road, facing east. c. 1908
Algarve Road is on the left.

The Leather Bottle Public House, Garratt Lane, looking west. c. 1912.

The earliest mention is in 1745, but it is probably earlier. Famous as the site of the election of the Mayor of Garratt between 1747 and 1796 when over 100,000 would gather for the mock election of various characters.

Beaumont Road, Southfields, looking north. c. 1910

Two little girls with their hoops in an oaken lane. The area was woodland into the late 1950s when Council Estates were placed here. Beaumont developed a major portion of land in the Southfields area. The Home for Incurables to the right of the trees.

Longfield Street, Southfields. c. 1912
Children could play in safety in the virtually deserted street. The boy on the right is wearing only one roller skate – probably sharing a pair with a friend.

Engadine Street, Southfields, facing east. c. 1912

Children gather for the photographer (R. J. Johns of Longley Road, Tooting – a prolific photographer of London street scenes). The little girl to the right of the delivery cycle carries her little sister forward to be in the scene. The delivery cycle bears the sign Edward Michael & Co., 62 Brookwood Road, Southfields.

Park Tavern Public House, Merton Road, Wandsworth, facing north. c. 1908

Horsedrawn buses from Wandsworth to Shepherds Bush using the area outside as a terminus whilst a constable keeps an eye on the situation. A peculiar point about Southfields is that when the owner of the land (a lady) sold the land for development in the 1880s, she put a covenant on the sale that no public houses were to be allowed in the area. Right to this day the covenant holds. The Park Tavern is just outside the 'no pub' zone and was the first to be built for the drinkers of Southfields. It stands at the lower end of West Hill Road, just on the left.

Trinity Road, Wandsworth Common, facing south. c. 1912

Four horsedrawn vehicles practically abreast in what appears to be an otherwise deserted street. Dorlcott Road is on the left of the picture and Alma Terrace on the right. The County Arms public house on the right was originally built in 1852 – one year after Wandsworth Prison at the back of the pub was opened. The pub was rebuilt in its present style in 1890.

Cicada Road, Wandsworth. c. 1906

The cast iron railings and gates which are still in place in this picture were removed during the Second World War for a scrap drive.

Wandsworth Infirmary, East Hill, looking south. c. 1906
What appears to be a businessman, striding purposefully to (or from) his place of work.

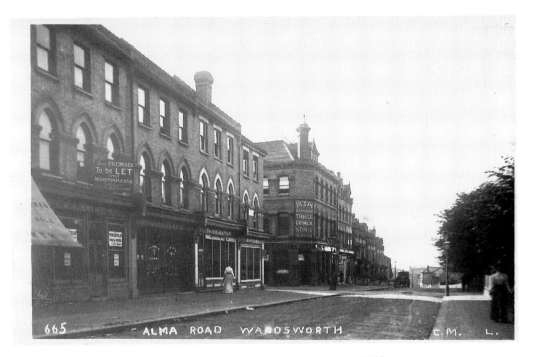

Alma Road, Wandsworth, facing north. c. 1908
The East Hill Hotel public house, proudly displaying the sign that it has on draught Reid's celebrated Three Guinea Stout.

Allfarthing Lane, Wandsworth, looking east at the junction of St. Ann's Park Road. c. 1906

(There never seems to be a shortage of children to pose for the photographer). The cart on the right of the group is delivering wet fish. Allfarthing is derived from Half Farthing, the name of the manor house which stood at the junction of Allfarthing Lane and St. Ann's Crescent.

Jeypore Road, Wandsworth. c. 1906

One wonders what the young lady is saying to distract the boys from their 'pose'. The small boy with the hoop, however, is determined to stand firm!

The Grove (now called St. Ann's Hill), looking north towards St. Ann's Hill School. c. 1906
Three delivery boys alone in the tree-lined road.

This is the Road I live in.

Baskerville Road, Wandsworth Common, facing south. c. 1906

Nicosia Road on the right. A late development in the 1870s on Wandsworth Common land, probably no further encroachment after this. Note the hand-written comment 'This is the road I live in' – which house, one wonders.

Fullerton Road, Wandsworth. c. 1912

Milk cart on the left and two ladies about to depart from their home on the right. Also on the right can be seen St. Faith's Church. The tower was demolished in October, 1967 after a 'Dangerous Structure Notice' was issued due to unsafe brickwork.

Wandsworth Prison Main Gates, Wandsworth Common. c. 1906

Built in 1851 as The Surrey House of Correction, it is the only prison in Britain to retain a condemned cell and gallows for the crime of treason or arson in naval dockyards. The prison can hold as many as 1,400 men.

Belle Vue Road, Wandsworth Common, facing west. c. 1908
A chilly winter scene with the Hope public house in the middle of the photograph on the corner of St. James' Drive.

'Cooling Their Tootsies' on Wandsworth Common. c. 1908

In complete contrast to the scene of No. 79.

Sheep on Wandsworth Common. c. 1908

A pastoral scene, probably three island pond alongside Bolingbroke Grove. Shepherds came down with flocks from Worcestershire and Northamptonshire and would feed the sheep on local heaths and common land before going on to the London meat markets.

Empire Day, St. Michael's Schools, Southfields. c. 1907

Children pose, proudly holding their Union Jacks, while teachers keep order and parents look on.

Wandle Schools, Garratt lane, Earlsfield, looking north. c. 1925
The school still stands.

Waldron Road Schools, Corner of Garratt Lane and Waldron Road, looking east. c. 1920
This was sadly lost due to bombing during the Second World War.

West Hill Infants School, Broomhill Road, Wandsworth, facing the east side of building. c. 1903

This imposing building is still in present use (1992). Of particular interest is the Presbytarian Church on the left, at the junction of Merton Road and Lebanon Gardens, which was bombed during World War II.

Swaffield Road Schools. c. 1906

Just a few of the pupils face the camera for this photograph.

CHURCH OF ST MICHAEL & ALL ANGELS SOUTHFIELDS

216D JOHNS

St. Michael and All Angels Church, Wimbledon Park Road, Southfields, looking north. c. 1912

The foundation stone was laid on 10th April, 1897 by Princess Mary Adelaide, Duchess of Teck. On completion of the building on 24th June, 1905, the memorial stone was laid by H.S.H. Prince Alexander George of Teck. The architect was E. W. Mountford, and the builders were W. Johnson & Co. Of interest is the open land on the right which was built upon with housing only a few years later.

Church of St. John the Divine, Garratt Lane, Earlsfield. Corner of Bendon Valley, looking south-west. c. 1912

Tin churches were built as temporary accommodation during the 1880s and 1890s and were usually replaced by stone buildings either on the site or alongside. It is not known if a church site was found elsewhere, but this corrugated iron church survived into the 1930s. It is, in fact, very rare to find a photograph of one of these buildings.

St. Andrew's Church, Garratt Lane, Earlsfield. c. 1912

The clock on the church in this picture was added in memory of King Edward VII who died in 1910.

Magdalen Road and Earlsfield Baptist Chapel, looking east. c. 1912

The only people to be seen are two ladies walking their dogs – probably an early-morning picture. Beyond the second road on the right, all the land was still allotments.

St. Ann's Church, St. Ann's Hill, Wandsworth, looking east. c. 1906

Known locally as 'The pepper-pot church' in view of the shape in which the tower was constructed.

St. Mary's Parish Church, Plough Lane, Summerstown, facing east. c. 1912

Opened on 30th April, 1904 and consecrated by the Bishop of Southwark, the church was built by Johnson & Co. of Wandsworth Common at a cost of £10,846. The architect was Godfrey Pinkerton.

The Mosque, Gressenhall Road, Southfields. c. 1926
This was Britain's first mosque and is still in use.

Garratt Lane, Earlsfield. c. 1915

Troops on the march (no 'cosy corner' for these men). In the background can be seen St. Andrew's Church.

Wandsworth Common, 1915

Training cadets of the Naval Wing of the Royal Flying Corps in piloting balloons. The R.N.A.S. had training facilities nearby at Roehampton and often flew in free flight balloons, for, when in observation balloons, they had to be capable of steering them if they broke loose from their moorings.

Southfields Peace Celebrations, Saturday, 19th July, 1919

At the junction of Replingham Road and Wimbledon Park Road – the vehicles of Goodley & Sons Ltd. taking prominence in the picture.